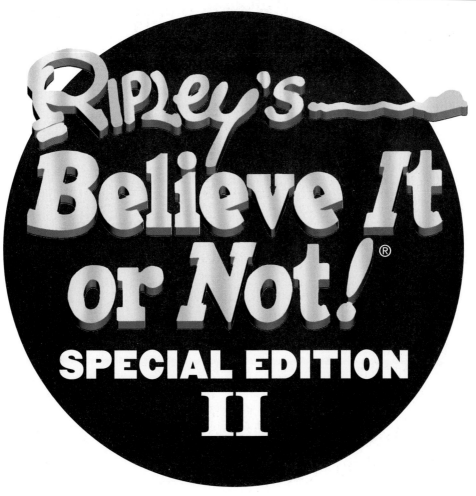

Ripley's Believe It or Not!®
SPECIAL EDITION
II

By Mary Packard
and the Editors of Ripley Entertainment Inc.

SCHOLASTIC INC.

New York   Toronto   London   Auckland   Sydney
Mexico City   New Delhi   Hong Kong   Buenos Aires

SMBSD

Developed by Nancy Hall, Inc.
Designed by Atif Toor
Cover design by Louise Bova
Photo research by Laura Miller
Index by Charles Carmony

ISBN 0-439-46554-0

12 11 10 9 8 7 6 5 4 3 2 1   5 6 7 8 9/0

Printed in the U.S.A.   40

First paperback printing, April 2005

CONTENTS

ROBERT RIPLEY'S WEIRD WORLD

Welcome to the weird and wonderful world of Robert Ripley. Ripley's Believe It or Not! is without question the most famous and enduring entertainment feature in all the world. For decades, more than 80 million people in 125 countries have been dazzled by Robert Ripley's incredible monument to the bizarre.

Robert Ripley visited a total of 201 countries, traveling a distance equal to 18 complete trips around the world. He delighted in learning about the customs of the people he met, and, if they were weird enough, he would feature them in his cartoons when he got back home.

Extra-odd-inary!

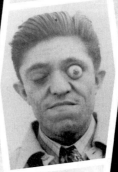

He's Got Mail

Robert Ripley got some of his best ideas from his fans. During the 1930s and '40s, Ripley received more than a million letters per year. That's 3,500 letters per day.

Album of the Odd

In the pages of this book you will meet some of the weirdest, wildest, most bizarre people in the world. Eric Sprague is trying his best to look like a reptile instead of a human. Avelino Perez got his kicks by popping his eyes right out their sockets. And for people like Dagmarr Rothman, swallowing a mouse was all in a day's work. Why do they do it? Only they know for sure!

RIPLEY FILES

Throughout this book, you'll find cartoons from the Ripley archives. The date that each cartoon was first published is shown at the top.

A Cache of Curios

Mummified cats, shrunken heads, and a ceremonial mask made from a human skull are just a few of the bizarre objects that have found their way into the Believe It or Not! collections.

BELIEVE IT!®

Often called the world's biggest liar, Robert Ripley said, "I don't blame anyone for thinking me a liar because there's nothing stranger than the truth."

Creature Features

Animals have a place in Ripley's world, too. Take Rollie, the penguin that was a member of the National Rollerskating Association. Or Mrs. W. R. Rhodes's dog, who liked to wear her owner's false teeth. Then there are the wild animals with strange habits and the animals that hold unusual jobs—all have been catalogued in the Ripley archives.

Strange Places

And when it comes to weird places, you'd have to go far to top the bone palace—which is made entirely of human bones. Unless, of course, you visit one of Ripley's own Odditoriums—museums dedicated to the showcasing of such oddities as a two-headed calf. Today, there are more than 26 Ripley Odditoriums in operation.

1

LET'S PARTY!

FESTIVALS, PARTIES, CELEBRATIONS, AND PASTIMES

Mess-tivals

Making a Splash

In India during the spring festival of Holi, partygoers mix a tinted powder called *gulal* with water and pour it into long tubes called *pichkaris*. The colored water flies through the air like liquid rainbows, making every human a target. Dumping buckets and pails of the stuff on passersby is also quite effective. Hysterical laughter can be heard everywhere, often drowning out the traditional cries of *"Bura na mano, Holi hai,"* which means "No harm intended, it's Holi!"

RIPLEY FILE: 6.20.54

Eating underwater! Once every year, 5,000 pilgrims come to Hatta, India, where they eat a full meal in the waters of a sacred pool. The pilgrims take a mouthful of food, then duck underwater to chew it up and swallow it.

TRUE GRIT

At the World Grits Festival in South Carolina, contestants get weighed before and after diving into a pool of grits. The person coated with the most grits wins.

Playing Dirty

Mud slinging is encouraged at the Mighty Mud Mania festival in Scottsdale, Arizona. Every July, kids of all ages slip and slide over mud-slathered ramps and crawl through muck-filled tunnels. More than 240,000 pounds of mud are used for this event!

Food Fight

Every August in the town of Buñol, Spain, 20,000 of its finest citizens start to see red. That's because they're celebrating the annual harvest with a festival called La Tomatina—which ends in the world's biggest tomato fight. The streets become slippery with splattered tomatoes. It isn't long before everyone looks like they've just taken a bath in marinara sauce.

Too Cool!

Seeing the Light

In the past, Chinese fishermen would carve lanterns out of blocks of ice to keep their candles from blowing out—a custom that inspired the Ice Lantern Festival held each year in Harbin, China. Ice sculptors carve figures of animals and people, as well as castles and pagodas, from thousands of blocks of ice. The sculptures are all lit from within by neon lights, creating a magical spectacle of bright, shimmering colors.

Chilly Reception

Visitors to the Winter Festival in Quebec, Canada, can stay in a hotel made entirely out of 11,350 tons of snow and ice. The hotel has a fireplace, two art galleries, a movie theater, a nearby skating rink—and even a wedding chapel! In the Ice Bar (above), beverages are refrigerated to keep them from freezing!

A SNOWBALL'S CHANCE

To celebrate Midsummer's Day in 2000, artist Andy Goldsworthy displayed 13 one-ton snowballs on the streets of London, England! He collected snow over two winters and had it kept in cold storage.

Thrills & Chills!

The second coldest capital city on Earth, Ottawa, Canada, hosts the Winterlude festival each year. Sculptors from all over the world arrive three weeks early, toting chain saws, picks, and axes, to carve giant figures of fanciful creatures, people, and buildings out of snow and huge blocks of ice.

Visitors can skate through a frozen maze, explore an ice castle, slide down the backs of huge sculptured animals, and watch movies at an outdoor theater with a 12-foot screen made out of snow.

They can also try out the world's longest skating rink—a five-mile stretch of the Rideau Canal, where as many as 100,000 people can glide along the ice at the same time!

Food Fest

Blue Plate Special

Film director Alfred Hitchcock (right) once threw a dinner party for actress Gertrude Lawrence. Guests were surprised by the menu, which featured food that was dyed blue, including peaches, trout, and ice cream!

Frankly Speaking

Eating hot dogs on the Fourth of July is a time-honored tradition. But who ever heard of eating more than 50 hot dogs in one sitting? In July 2002, twenty-four-year-old Takeru, "the Tsunami," Kobayashi (left) of Japan ate $50\frac{1}{2}$ hot dogs in just 12 minutes during the 87th Annual Nathan's Famous Hot Dog Eating Contest in Coney Island, New York. Not only did he win the coveted Mustard Yellow Belt for the second year in a row, he also beat his previous world record by half a hot dog.

What an eggs-aggeration! An omelet made with 7,200 eggs was cooked in a pan eight feet across. It weighed half a ton! The pan was greased by girls skating across it with slabs of bacon attached to their feet!

Bun-anza

Seymour, Wisconsin, was once home to the Hamburger Hall of Fame and the annual Burger Fest, which featured a bun toss, a ketchup slide, and a hamburger parade. In 2001, Seymour set a world's record when it grilled an 8,266-pound hamburger!

A LOTTA BREAD

Six chefs at a hotel in Tokyo, Japan, used 14,000 pieces of bread to create a ten-foot-tall replica of Godzilla that weighed 1,000 pounds.

Isn't It Romantic?

The most dazzling procession in history! In 1406, the wedding party at the marriage of the daughter of King Deva Raya I of Vijayanagar, India, to Sultan Firoz Shah of Kulbarga, walked from the city gate to the royal palace—a distance of six miles—on a carpet of gold cloth.

Bad Hair Days

Many ancient marriage rituals were all about hair. At Russian weddings, the bride's hair was sprinkled with a mixture of oats, barley, and linseed oil. In Abyssinia, locks of the bride's and groom's hair were dipped in honey and water and glued to each other's head. In ancient Rome, the groom combed the bride's hair with his spear to frighten away evil spirits.

WHAT A YOLK!

Forget about rice. At weddings during the Middle Ages, people showered newly married couples with eggs!

Bridal Sweet

At Salon du Chocolat in Tokyo, Japan, a chocolate fashion show featured a wedding gown trimmed with pink chocolate hearts and bows (right). Created by Japanese fashion designer Yumi Katsura and chocolatier Koji Tsuchiya, this dress *is* good enough to eat!

Mass-trimony

About 3,500 couples from 186 countries were married on February 16, 2002, at the Olympic stadium in Seoul, South Korea (above). An even bigger wedding took place there in 1995, when 35,000 couples tied the knot at the same time!

Party Spirits

Guiding Lights

According to Chinese tradition, the ghosts of the dead return to Earth to visit their relatives during Ghost Month. At the Keelung Ghost Day Festival in Taiwan, lanterns on top of bamboo poles as tall as 60 feet are used to call the ghosts to a feast, and water lanterns up to two stories tall are released in Wanghai Harbor (right) to lure the water spirits. At the end of Ghost Month, a Taoist monk raises a "seven-star" sword to chase reluctant ghosts back to the underworld.

BAD GROOMING

On November 16, 1667, Dorothy Ford was married to William Streat of South Pool, England. What was so unusual about that? The bridegroom was a corpse!

The Tell-Tale Toast

The grave of Edgar Allan Poe in Baltimore, Maryland, has been visited each year since 1949 on January 19, Poe's birthday. A loyal mystery guest places a bouquet of roses and a bottle of cognac on the novelist's grave. The cognac bottle is always open, with one drink taken.

Skulls and Bones

In Mexico, it is said, "We are not here for a long time—we are here for a good time." Many Mexicans believe that the dead return once a year to visit with their loved ones. To make them feel welcome, relatives celebrate the Day of the Dead on the first two days in November, decorating graves of deceased relatives with flowers and candles. The Day of the Dead is one of the happiest days of the year, celebrated with puppets, masks, skull candies, and skeletons, of course.

RIPLEY FILE: 11.10.60

Dance till you drop! In the Kapsiki tribe of Africa, a wealthy person who dies is given a head start on the good life that Kapsikis believe a person of standing should live in the next world. The village blacksmith hoists the corpse on his shoulders and gives it dancing lessons that last for hours!

Extra! Extra!

TECHNO-PHOBIA

At the annual da Vinci Days Festival in Corvallis, Oregon, people used to toss things—even computers and household appliances—from a giant catapult!

FOWL FESTIVITIES

At the annual Wayne Chicken Show held in July, residents of Wayne, Nebraska, can choose from a variety of events. For winged contestants, there is a Best Chicken Song contest and a Most Beautiful Beak contest. Humans can compete in the Rubber Chicken Olympics or the National Cluck-Off contest—the person who sounds and acts the most like a chicken wins!

HOT STUFF

Residents of Patzcuaro, Mexico, celebrate the New Year by playing a game similar to hockey, except they use a burning ball of rags for a puck!

DOO-TY CALLS

Participants at the annual Moose Dropping Festival in Talkeetna, Alaska, watch as a hot-air balloon dumps 1,000 numbered pieces of moose poop. The person whose piece lands closest to an X etched on the ground wins $1,000.

SHABBY CHIC

Susan Lane of Toluca Lake, California, created a wedding dress and bouquet out of recycled trash including plastic bags, egg cartons, and cotton balls.

HEAD TRIP

Ordered to go to war on his wedding day, Prince Khalid of India killed himself after directing that his head be cut off and sent to his fiancée. The marriage was performed on schedule.

BIG KISS-OFF

In 1999, in the Republic of Belarus in eastern Europe, 6,000 people smacked their lips as they took part in a simultaneous Valentine's Day kiss.

FRUITS AND NUTS

Every January, the Great Fruitcake Toss is held in Manitou Springs Memorial Park in Colorado. Participants have a grand old time, swatting their unwanted Christmas fruitcakes with baseball bats, hitting them with golf clubs, flinging them from catapults, and hurling them from rooftops, while fellow party goers cheer them on. Some people might say the fruitcakes are getting their just desserts!

DOG DAYS

In New Orleans, Louisiana, the annual Mardi Gras celebration is not just for people. Dogs get to dress up, too—and they get to show off their duds when they walk in their very own costume parade.

BACKTRACKING

On one special holiday in Fort Wayne, Indiana, it's hard to tell who's coming and who's going. That's because residents celebrate Backwards Day by wearing their clothes backwards and walking backwards!

GETTING ANTSY

Since fire ants are almost impossible to get rid of, the folks in Marshall, Texas, have decided to make the best of things by hosting the Fire Ant Festival. Every year, about 50,000 people come to participate in such activities as the Fire Ant Call, a live Fire Ant Roundup, and the Fire Ant Chili & Bean Cook-off, which requires at least one fire ant to be part of each dish.

SWING YOUR TRACTOR

Believe It or Not! Tractor square dancing is a popular pastime at parties in Iowa! Farmers tour the countryside promenading and do-si-do-ing on vintage tractors!

21

2

PAST TENSE

AMAZING DISCOVERIES AND HYSTERICAL HISTORY

Under Wraps

Golden Oldie

The tomb of King Tutankhamun ("King Tut"), who ruled Egypt from 1361 to 1352 B.C.E., was discovered in 1922. Inside were thousands of treasures. A solid gold coffin contained the king's mummy. A large gold mask, inlaid with jewels and protected by magic spells, guarded his head.

Stuffed Animal

In ancient Egypt, cats were considered sacred. Some were mummified and buried with their owners, but cats also had their own tombs and burial grounds.

Tut's Guts

To make a mummy, Egyptian embalmers used 400 pounds of natron salt and 150 yards of linen. The body organs were removed, individually wrapped with linen strips, and placed in four canopic jars, whose lids were fashioned to represent different gods.

TIC-TAC-TOE

Archaeologists discovered a 3,000-year-old mummy with an artificial big toe. Attached with linen strings, the toe had scuff marks on the bottom, proving that its owner had walked around on it.

Ghost Town

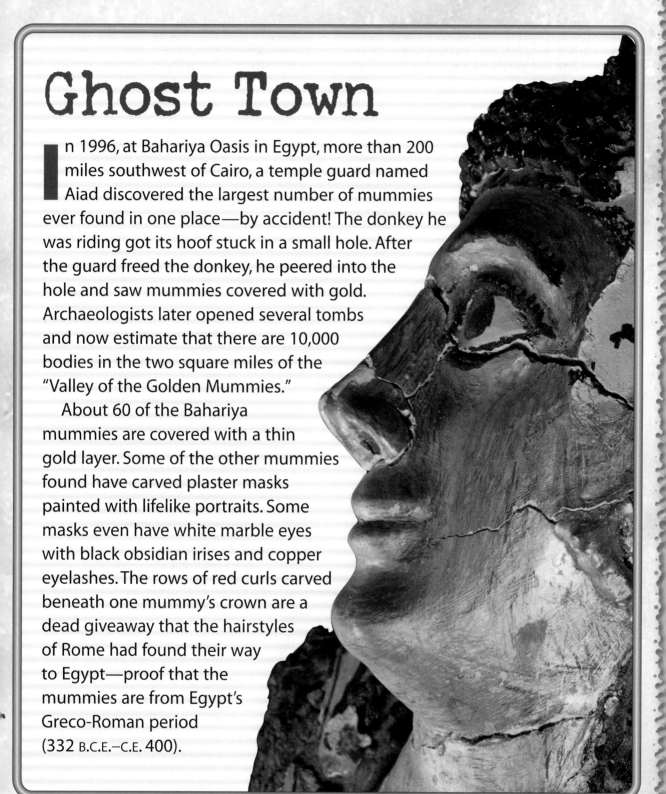

I n 1996, at Bahariya Oasis in Egypt, more than 200 miles southwest of Cairo, a temple guard named Aiad discovered the largest number of mummies ever found in one place—by accident! The donkey he was riding got its hoof stuck in a small hole. After the guard freed the donkey, he peered into the hole and saw mummies covered with gold. Archaeologists later opened several tombs and now estimate that there are 10,000 bodies in the two square miles of the "Valley of the Golden Mummies."

About 60 of the Bahariya mummies are covered with a thin gold layer. Some of the other mummies found have carved plaster masks painted with lifelike portraits. Some masks even have white marble eyes with black obsidian irises and copper eyelashes. The rows of red curls carved beneath one mummy's crown are a dead giveaway that the hairstyles of Rome had found their way to Egypt—proof that the mummies are from Egypt's Greco-Roman period (332 B.C.E.–C.E. 400).

Under Cover

On Another Note...

In her day, Josephine Baker (left) was as famous as Madonna. Perhaps that's why no one suspected she was a spy. During World War II, she smuggled secret messages throughout Europe, written in invisible ink on her sheet music.

Native Tongue

Risking their lives on the front lines during World War II, Navajo marines called "code talkers" translated orders transmitted to them in Navajo—a difficult language guaranteed to stump the enemy! For their heroic efforts, they finally received Congressional Medals of Honor in 2001.

Top Secret

Elizabeth "Crazy Bet" Van Lew was considered eccentric by many, but during the Civil War, she ran a spy ring composed of slaves and free people who worked as servants, farmers, seamstresses, storekeepers, and undercover abolitionists.

HOME RUN!

During World War II, American baseball player Moe Berg was the spy who learned that Germany did not have an atomic bomb—delivering information crucial to the Allies' strategy.

RIPLEY FILE: 6.06.68

The spy who would not quit! After losing a leg in the French retreat from Moscow, Russia, Captain Herman Lemaire still delivered secret dispatches to Napoleon. He dressed himself in beggar's clothing and, on a hastily fitted wooden leg, walked from Hamburg, Germany, to Paris, France—a distance of 600 miles!

Tools of the Trade

With a dog-doo transmitter (above) for a homing device, a spy did not have to worry that anyone would tamper with the equipment. The escape-and-evasion scarf was another useful tool. This one made a fashion statement while also providing the wearer with lifesaving escape routes embedded in the fabric.

Can You Dig It?

A Lot of Dough!

The world's oldest bakery was discovered by archaeologists in 1991 in Giza, Egypt. Equipped with a hearth, mixing vats, and bell-shaped bread pots called *bedja*, the 4,600-year-old bakery probably helped feed the more than 20,000 workers who built the nearby pyramids and the Sphinx.

Mammoth Tale

The Imperial mammoth was one of the largest land mammals that ever lived. Neanderthal men and women ate its meat, wore its skin, used its oily bones to keep their fires burning, and even used its tusks to fasten roofs to their dwellings.

Heavenly Snack

Archaeologists in Peru found sealed vases in the arms of entombed bodies dating back to 1500 B.C.E. The vases were filled with peanuts that were still edible!

In 1952, in Oconto, Wisconsin, 13-year-old Donald Baldwin discovered a prehistoric burial ground of the Copper Culture people, complete with forged copper implements such as awls, spear points, and fishhooks.

RIPLEY FILE: 10.29.50

The first taxicab in history! Archaeologists unearthed a 2,000-year-old horse-drawn carriage in Rome. The carriage was equipped with a meter that dropped pebbles into a drum when a rear wheel revolved. The number of pebbles determined the fare.

Head Trip

Evidence of brain surgery has been found in skulls dating back to the Stone Age—almost 7,000 years ago.

Presidential Trivia

Say Cheese!

By the time George Washington was 57 years old, he may have had only one natural tooth left—but he had six sets of dentures. They were made from the teeth of human cadavers, cows, elk, and even a rhinoceros. No wonder he rarely smiled!

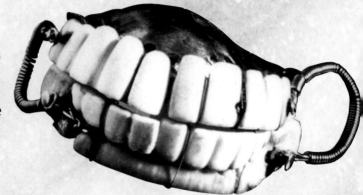

A Howling Good Time

President Lyndon B. Johnson had two beagles named Him and Her. He also had a stray mutt that he called Yuki. For laughs, he taught Yuki to "sing," and from time to time, he would join the dog in a howlingly good duet.

Rough Rider

A fanatic shot Theodore Roosevelt in the right lung during his 1912 campaign for the presidency. Nevertheless, Roosevelt made a scheduled campaign speech a few hours later, saying, "There is a bullet in my body, but it takes more than that to kill a bull moose!"

One day, reporter Anne Royall caught President John Quincy Adams skinny-dipping in the Potomac River. She sat on his clothes and refused to budge until he agreed to an interview.

RIPLEY FILE: 4.19.76

The president has a ball! At the April 14, 1910, baseball game between the Washington Senators and the Philadelphia Athletics, President William Howard Taft started the custom of throwing out the first ball of the year.

Track Star

At a crowded railroad station in the early 1860s, Abraham Lincoln's son Robert (above right) slipped feetfirst between the train and the platform. He was saved by Edwin Booth (above left), the brother of John Wilkes Booth—who would later assassinate Robert's father!

Gotcha!

Dead Wrong

In 1999, ads announced The Final Curtain, a chain of memorial theme parks. Clients could have their remains displayed in whatever creative way they wished—for instance, one person specified that his ashes be mixed with iron filings and placed in a giant Etch-A-Sketch. A year after the ads appeared, The Final Curtain was revealed as a hoax designed to protest the commercialization of the funeral industry.

Skullduggery

Charles Dawson and Arthur Woodward claimed a skull that they found near Piltdown, England, was half a million years old. The "Piltdown man" was accepted as authentic for 30 years—until scientists discovered it had the teeth and jawbone of a modern ape!

Fairy Fever

In 1917, Elsie Wright photographed tiny "fairies" dancing for her cousin, Frances Griffiths. Sir Arthur Conan Doyle, author of the Sherlock Holmes novels, published the photo with a story, which many people took as proof that fairies existed. Not until 1982 did Wright and Griffiths admit to faking the photograph.

In 1975, Nature Magazine published Sir Peter Scott and Alan Wilkins's scientific name for Scotland's Loch Ness Monster, Nessiteras rhombopteryx—which is also an anagram for "Monster Hoax by Sir Peter S"!

Mars Attack!

In 1938, Orson Welles aired a radio broadcast of "War of the Worlds," a story by H. G. Wells, using realistic news bulletins to announce unfolding events. Although Welles began the program with a statement that the broadcast was fictional drama, many listeners panicked, convinced that Martians really were invading Earth!

RIPLEY FILE: 12.03.39

The tablets of history!

Emperor Ch'in Shih Huang Ti (builder of the Great Wall of China) ordered the destruction of all literature and the execution of all historians so that history might begin with him! Fortunately, he overlooked the Stone Tablets of Beijing, on which Chinese history was engraved.

Extra! Extra!

GET THE HOOK?

A rare species of fur-bearing trout was caught in Lake Superior. It is believed that the extremely frigid water temperatures caused this fish to grow its dense coat of white fur. *Not!* Actually, the fur was glued to the trout by Ross Jobe of Ontario, Canada, who hoped to make a killing by selling it as a rare specimen!

BRIGHT HOUSE

Benjamin Harrison was th first president to have electricity in the White House. But after he got an electrical shock, he and hi family were afraid to touc the light switches and often went to bed with all the lights blazing.

SMOKE AND MIRRORS

Archimedes, a scientist of ancient Greece, saved the city of Syracuse from attack by Roman ships by setting fire to the ships—using huge mirrors and the sun.

HANDY VICTORY

In 1015 B.C.E., Heremon O'Neill had a boating rac with a rival chieftain. The first man to touch its soil would rule Ireland. O'Neil won by cutting off his hand and hurling it to shore, a sacrifice that mad him the first king of Ulste

CHEW CHEW TREE

Archaeologists discovered the world's oldest chewing gum in Sweden—a 9,000-year-old piece of birch resin with teeth marks in it.

GOING OUT IN STYLE

Scientists in Ladby, Denmark, uncovered a 1,000-year-old Viking warship that held the body of a Viking warrior, buried with his weapons, his favorite hunting dogs, and 12 horses.

SILENT PARTNER

Unlike most politicians, President Calvin Coolidge didn't much like the sound of his own voice. When a dinner guest bet that he could get him to say more than two words, he replied, "You lose."

BARKER-IN-CHIEF

President Richard Nixon once worked as a carnival barker!

ROUND AND ROUND SHE GOES...

MONKEY BUSINESS

In 1842, a lot of people were fooled when P. T. Barnum exhibited a creation he called "The Feejee Mermaid." Later in the 19th century, gullible tourists in the South Pacific bought similar "mermaids," which were made from the front of a dried-up monkey corpse attached to the back of a fish.

CHEEKY ADVICE

Abraham Lincoln grew his beard on the advice of Grace Bedell, an 11-year-old girl from Westfield, New York. In a letter that was dated October 15, 1860, she wrote, "If you would let your whiskers grow ... you would look a great deal better for your face is so thin. All the ladies like whiskers ... and then you would be president."

GOLD TOAST

Once a year for the last 672 years, the mayor of Grammot, Belgium, and every member of his town council, has been required to drink a cup of wine containing a live goldfish!

BONE OF CONTENTION

An old law in Chicago, Illinois, made it illegal to take a French poodle to the opera.

3

DISORDER
IN THE COURT

WEIRD LAWS AND STUPID CRIMINALS

On the Books

Half-baked

In 17th-century England, Oliver Cromwell banned pies, which he thought were an extravagance. At one time in Wisconsin, it was illegal to serve apple pie without cheese. And an old law in Tennessee stated that anyone ordering pie in a restaurant had better eat the whole thing right there.

How Dog-matic!

At one time in Normal, Oklahoma, making an ugly face at a dog could get you arrested. An old Minnesota law made it illegal for cats to chase dogs up telephone poles. And at one time in Berea, Ohio, dogs and cats outside after dark had to wear taillights.

MAKING A SPLASH

In Hanford, California, kids can jump in mud puddles to their hearts' content because it's against the law for anyone to stop them.

Arresting Moments

In Santa Ana, California, it's illegal to swim on dry land. In West Virginia, sneezing on a train is forbidden, as is drinking milk on a train passing through North Carolina. And whatever you do, don't step off a plane while it's flying over Maine—you could be arrested!

RIPLEY FILE: 2.15.42

Trial of the fleas! **After a plague of fleas in 1670, the high court of Munster, Germany, summoned the insects to appear before it. Every flea but one disobeyed and were therefore banished for ten years.**

Loony Lawbreakers

Hot Cross Buns

In May 2001, a man was arrested in Paris, France, for trying to put out the "eternal flame" under the Arc de Triomphe (below) by sitting on it. Before he could be put in jail, he had to be taken to the hospital to be treated for burns on his butt.

Working Off-the-Books

A man robbing a late-night convenience store in Florida found only $50 in the cash register. To boost his take, he locked the clerks in the freezer and waited on customers for three hours. Unfortunately for him, two of the regular customers he served were local policemen!

Calling All Thieves

Police investigating a burglary decided to try the number of a pager that had been stolen. It went off in the pocket of a man standing nearby—who was being questioned about a completely different crime.

In the late 1700s, a London thief picked the pocket of Judge John Silvester while being found not guilty of picking other pockets! He later confessed and returned the judge's watch.

RIPLEY FILE: 01.01.78

When crime stood still! Among the many citizens of Pompeii who were petrified forever when volcanic mud spewed from Mount Vesuvius and buried them was a man defending his riches with a sword. Around his still-standing figure lay the petrified bodies of five would-be thieves.

Deposit Drama

In 1997, a 61-year-old woman was waiting for her receipt at the drive-in window of a bank in New Mexico when police roared up and ordered her out of the car at gunpoint. It turned out her deposit slip had a holdup note on the back. The FBI discovered that a prankster had written the note and left the slip to be picked up by an unsuspecting customer.

And Justice for All

Tooth or Consequences

At one time in South Foster, Rhode Island, if a dentist extracted the wrong tooth from a patient, he was ordered by law to have one of his own teeth extracted by the local blacksmith.

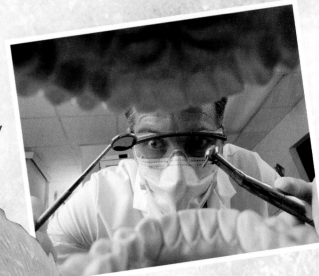

Winged Victory

When a stolen parrot in New Delhi, India, was brought to court as a witness, it identified its real owner by repeating the names of her children.

—Leena!
—Sangeeta!
—Rajiv!

In ancient China, a suspect being questioned in court had to chew and spit out a handful of rice powder—if the powder stayed dry, the suspect was considered guilty!

Tit for Tat

In 1992, Judge Brown of Memphis, Tennessee, allowed victims of robberies to take anything they wanted from the home of the thief who had robbed them! And that same year, a judge in Newark, New Jersey, sentenced a landlord to live in his own run-down apartment building.

Crocodile Tears

Attorney Carl Harper of Bedias, Texas, had a secret weapon—a handkerchief filled with chopped onions! He may not have smelled very good, but he won most of his cases because, more often than not, his flowing tears won the sympathy of the jury.

RIPLEY FILE: 12.27.42

Paid in kind! Jean de la Balue invented the "Iron Cage"—a torture chamber in which the prisoner could neither stand up nor stretch out—and was the first man imprisoned in it! He spent 11 years in his own cage.

Extra! Extra!

SCHOOL DAZE

In medieval England, it was illegal not to play hooky! Peasants were fined if they sent their children to school instead of making them work in the fields.

LAW AND ORDER

Paule Viguier (1518–161◼ of Toulouse, France, was ◼ beautiful that the people ◼ rioted when she remaine◼ indoors for several days. The city adopted a law requiring Viguier to appear on her balcony twice each day—which she did until her death at the age of ninety-two.

PRETTY FISHY

There was once a time in Alaska when you could be arrested if you stuck out your tongue at someone who caught a smaller fish than you did.

A-RESTING ATMOSPHERE

The courtroom of Judge Roberto Portugal in Curitiba, Brazil, features aromatherapy, soothing music, and walls that have been painted in calming colors.

STYLE FILE

In Chicago, Illinois, it's illegal to go fishing while wearing pajamas. In Carmel, New York, a man can't go out wearing a jacket that doesn't match his pants. And in Thailand, you can't leave the house without putting on your underwear.

NOT SO FREE TIME

On the island of Jersey, England, it's illegal for a man to knit during fishing season. And in Fremont, California, repairing spacecraft in your garage is against the law.

PHOTO FINISH

Two Chicago thieves left behind a camera when they burgled a house. The owner had the film developed—and found that it contained a photo that one of the thieves had taken of the other.

DO NOT DISTURB

The city of Port Henry, New York, has passed a law forbidding anyone from disturbing the sea creature that was believed to live in Lake Champlain.

PANT-A-LOONIES

Horses are not allowed in the town of Fountain Inn, South Carolina, unless they are wearing pants!

KNEE-JERK RESPONSE

In 1807, Czar Alexander I of Russia ordered his troops to stop and check all carriages for men wearing long trousers. Any man found wearing them would have his legs cut off at the knee.

NIT-PICKLING

In Boston, Massachusetts, any pickle for sale must be able to bounce four inches when dropped from waist height.

CALL THE PET POLICE

In Detroit, Michigan, it's illegal to tie your pet crocodile to a fire hydrant. You can't own a dog in Beijing, China, but you can rent one—at a rate of 23 cents for ten minutes. In Wilbur, Washington, don't get caught riding an ugly horse because it's against the law!

4

AGAINST
ALL ODDS

NATURAL DISASTERS AND AMAZING ESCAPES

Blasting Off

Hot Stuff

Seconds after Mount Saint Helens exploded in May 1980, Jim Scymanky (left), a logger working ten miles away, was engulfed by a cloud of red-hot ash. Though badly burned, he was the only one of his crew to survive.

Rocking and Rolling

With little warning, the Philippine volcano Mayon (above) erupted on July 26, 2002, blasting out fiery ash and sending rocks the size of cars rolling down its slopes at speeds of 60 miles per hour. More than 40,000 people fled their homes but, amazingly, not one person was killed!

IMAGINE THAT!

The eruption of Mount Saint Helens created enough ash and dust to cover an island the size of Manhattan to a depth of 28 stories.

They Blew Their Stacks!

In 1880, molten lava flowed from Mauna Loa (below) for six months, halting just a half mile before reaching the city of Hilo, more than 30 miles away! Many Hawaiians claimed that it stopped because the Princess Kamahameha threw a lock of her hair into the fiery mass. When Mauna Loa erupted again in 1935, the 23rd Bomb Squadron of the U.S. Army used twenty 600-pound bombs to change the direction of the lava flow and once again saved Hilo from destruction.

On February 20, 1943, the ground in Dionisio Pulido's cornfield in Mexico cracked open, spewing gas and smoke. By dusk, the fissure was spitting hot cinders. Within 24 hours, a cone had risen to 160 feet, and within a week, it was more than 300 feet tall. Named after a nearby village, the new volcano, Paricutín, stood 1,100 feet above its base within a year.

Out of the Blue

Swept Away

In 1997, Virginia Davidson of Jarrell, Texas, took refuge in her bathtub and waited for a tornado to pass through. Before she knew it, she was swept into the air, then set down in a field, right in the middle of a mud puddle. The bathtub was nowhere in sight.

RIPLEY FILE: 1.12.41

The strangest story of the sea!
In 1907, when a meteor struck the sailing ship *Eclipse* in the mid-Pacific, the masts were carried away and the vessel was abandoned. All but three on board escaped in lifeboats and rowed 900 miles to Hawaii in 13 days.

RECYCLING

In 1936, a hen owned by J. D. Rucker was trapped in a crate when a tornado devastated the town of Gainesville, Georgia. It was rescued 47 days later, having survived by eating its own eggs.

Home Wrecker

A tornado carried away one end of a house (above) without disturbing the dishes in the pantry.

Windfall

On October 9, 1992, Michelle Knapp of Peekskill, New York, heard a loud bang. She raced outside and found the trunk of her car caved in (above). Underneath was a large, foul-smelling meteorite (right)! Knapp was delighted when collectors paid her $10,000 for her 12-year-old jalopy and more than $50,000 for the meteorite.

Nature's Fury

Homespun

During a winter storm, a cottage in Malagash Point, Canada, was lifted from its foundation and set down a quarter mile away. Amazingly, everything inside remained intact—even the bottles on top of a kitchen cabinet.

On Board

In 1868, Holoua, a resident of Kauai, Hawaii, whose home was swept out to sea by a tidal wave, saved himself by tearing a plank from the wall and riding it back to shore. This event was recorded in Honolulu as the highest wave ever surfed.

RUB-A-DUB-DUB

In a flood that destroyed her family's house, nine-year-old Amber Colvin of Shadyside, Ohio, survived by riding inside a bathtub down the Ohio River.

RIPLEY FILE: 12.10.60

Unidentified survivor! A box lashed to a crude raft washed up on the beach at Provincetown, Massachusetts. Inside was an infant, the only survivor of a ship that sank in a storm. The child was adopted by a mariner and called George Sopter, but he never learned his true name, his real nationality, or even the name of the ship.

Moving Experience

In Pennsylvania, a 12-room house was carried away by the Johnstown flood of May 31, 1889. It was deposited two miles away, on a foundation laid for a house that was being built from identical blueprints by the same contractor. William Thomas, owner of the property, bought the house and lived there for 43 years.

Up on the Rooftop

In 1986, cows that were caught in a raging flood in Kansas climbed up on the rooftops of submerged houses and stayed there until they were rescued.

Wreck and Ruin

Shipping News

On July 25, 1956, two ships, the *Andrea Doria* and the *MV Stockholm,* collided. In one of the most amazing rescues in maritime history, five ships answered the distress call and rescued 1,654 passengers. Survivor Ann Mackenzie (below) smiled in relief after learning that her mother was also among the passengers who were saved.

RIPLEY FILE: 1.01.78

Dead man's controls! Automatic brakes were installed in all New Jersey passenger trains after the Bayonne disaster of 1958, when a commuter train plunged off an open drawbridge and 48 people drowned in Newark Bay. It was believed that, at the moment the train reached the warning lights, the engineer and fireman suffered simultaneous heart attacks!

Track Meet

Seconds after a car slid down an embankment and onto the railroad tracks in Selby, England, a passenger train traveling at 125 miles per hour crashed into it. The train then hit an oncoming freight train carrying 1,000 tons of coal. Miraculously, most of the 100 passengers survived.

Heavy Metal

Jack Thompson, as featured in a wax figure display (below), survived a car accident in which a metal pole ripped through his chest.

WAY TO GO!

In 1952, a stock car finished first in a race even after its wheels came off. It flipped over and skidded upside down across the finish line.

Lucky Breaks

Up, Up, and Away

Eight-year-old Deandra Anrig (right) was flying her brand-new 12-foot-wide kite in Mountain View, California, when a twin-engine plane caught the kite's nylon line. The airplane lifted the little girl off the ground and carried her 100 feet before she let go—just in time to avoid smashing into a very large tree.

Up Close and Personal

Ten visitors at the Aquarium of the Americas in New Orleans, Louisiana, got a closer look than they bargained for when a catwalk split in two, plunging them into a 20-foot-deep, 400,000-gallon tank filled with sharks and stingrays. The tourists, including a two-year-old, thrashed in panic for 15 minutes until they were rescued. No one was seriously injured.

Bumper Sticker

Three-year-old Chelsea Tafoya survived without injuries after clinging to the windshield wipers on the back window of her father's SUV for almost 12 miles while he sped along at up to 83 miles per hour. Finally, a passing motorist caught her father's attention, and he stopped.

ON TRACK

In 1919, a storage tank in Boston, Massachusetts, burst, spewing two million gallons of hot molasses and collapsing an elevated railway. Luckily, an approaching train stopped just in time to avoid a sticky doom.

RIPLEY FILE: 8.24.58

Saved by her hair! Caroline Homassel, was trapped inside a theater that was on fire in Richmond, Virginia. Her braids were so long that Dr. Philip Thornton, who was trapped with her, was able to use them to lower her safely to the ground! Homassel then summoned help for her rescuer—and later married him!

Hole-y Terror

A pilot flew his biplane 275 miles and landed safely—after it was riddled with 4,700 holes made by hailstones the size of baseballs!

Extra! Extra!

SCRAPE GOAT

The driver of a two-ton ice-cream truck that went flying 215 feet down a hill and into a tree in Reelsville, Indiana, was a nanny goat!

HOW CRUSHING

In 1994, a truck in Areny de Mar, Spain, was hit by a car, pushed onto a railroad track, and crushed by an oncoming train. The truck's driver and passenger walked away from the wreck with minor injuries.

MANHOLE DIET

On his way to buy some fast food, high school teacher Kevin Funchess fell into a manhole in a grassy area beneath the freeway near his home. He was wedged in so tightly that he couldn't reach into his backpack to answer the calls that worried family members kept making to his cell phone. Funchess remained stuck in the hole until, after three days without food and water, he was able to shift his body to get to his phone and dial for help.

LUCKY SLIP-UP

In 1859, Sarah Ann Henley survived falling 250 feet from the Clifton Suspension Bridge in England when her petticoat opened up like a parachute, breaking her fall.

MILK SHAKE

During a snowstorm in 1898 near Fitchburg, Massachusetts, a two-car milk train crashed head-on into a locomotive, landing on top of it—but no one on board was seriously injured.

GOING BUGGY

Nine-month-old Sara Gillies of Perth, Australia, survived inside her baby carriage after it was hit and dragged under an oncoming train!

ON GUARD

A fisherman from the Province of Kein Giang, Vietnam, survived after being stabbed by a swordfish. The two-foot-long sword entered through his forehead and exited to the right of his cervical vertebrae.

FALL GUY

At age five, Nicholas Fagnani fell 55 feet and lived. At 12, he survived a 20-story fall from the Liberty Bank Building in Buffalo, New York. At the age of 24, he was hit by a train, thrown 300 feet into the air, and—you guessed it—survived!

THE HUMAN PIPE CLEANER

In 1989, William Lamm of Vero Beach, California, escaped unhurt after being sucked into a water pipe and traveling though it for 1,500 feet at 50 miles per hour!

BRANDED!

In 1968, a bolt of lightning tattooed a man with the initials of a doctor whom he had once robbed. Even more amazing, the man was revived by that very same doctor who had just happened to be on the scene.

HAPPY LANDING

On January 6, 1983, Keung Ng of Massachusetts was asleep in his fourth-floor apartment when an explosion destroyed the building. Still in bed, Ng fell down three flights, landed on a pile of debris, then got up and walked away.

BEGINNER'S LUCK

Two-year-old Michael Collins of Pennsylvania drove his mother's car over a guardrail, down a 54-foot embankment, and across a four-lane highway—yet escaped without injury!

MONEY TO BURN

In January of 1990, Canadians Don Wing and Jack Joneson got lost while skiing at Big Mountain Resort in Montana. They survived the extreme cold by burning dollar bills!

CLIFFHANGERS

In 1953, seven Japanese acrobats survived a highway accident by diving out of the windows when their bus skidded off a cliff.

5

BODY
LANGUAGE

MEDICAL MARVELS, MYSTERIES, AND CURIOSITIES

From Head to Toe

Thumbs-up

According to a recent study, using high-tech gadgets, such as cell phones and handheld video games (below), has caused a physical mutation in today's youth. Research in nine cities around the world shows that the thumbs of people under age 25 have replaced the index finger as the most useful digit.

Brain Power

Research in Britain suggests that you can get into shape just by thinking about it! Eighteen subjects were divided into three groups. The first group exercised their little fingers twice a week. The second group just thought about exercising, and the third group did nothing. The first group increased pinky strength by 33 percent and the third group remained the same. However, pinkies in the second group got 16 percent stronger! Why? Increased brain activity sent faster signals to the muscles, improving performance.

Buggin' Out

Did you know that, as you read this, 8,000 bacteria are camping out on each square inch of your legs? If that's not enough to make your skin crawl, you may be interested to know that at any given time nearly two million bacteria call your face home!

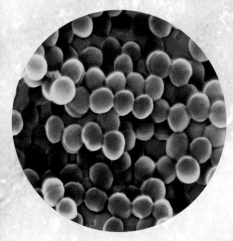

HEART-THROBS

In 75 years, the human heart pumps more than three billion gallons of blood—enough to fill an oil tanker 46 times!

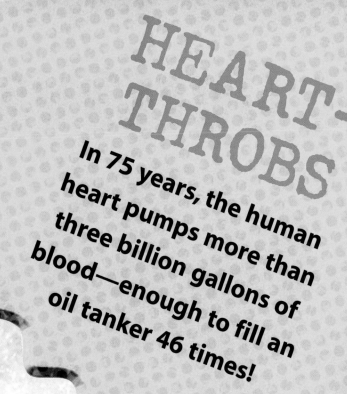

For All You're Worth

The human body has a net worth of about $4.50! That's the monetary value of its elements—including oxygen, carbon, hydrogen, and calcium, as well as the traces of gold found in toenails.

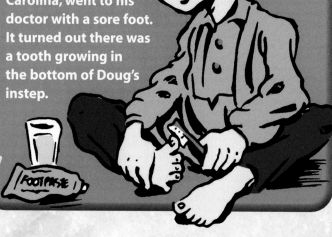

**RIPLEY FILE:
10.01.90**

Misplaced tooth!
In 1978, Doug Pritchard, age 13, of Lenoir, North Carolina, went to his doctor with a sore foot. It turned out there was a tooth growing in the bottom of Doug's instep.

Curious Cures

Taters for Tots

Soon kids may be able to eat french fries instead of getting shots! Scientists are altering the genes of potatoes to give them built-in vaccines. At Loma Linda Medical School in California, a potato with a built-in vaccine for cholera—a disease that kills three million children a year—has been successfully tested on mice. This could greatly benefit children who live in poor countries and can't afford expensive vaccines.

RIPLEY FILE: 1.01.50

Low-tech bug light! In 1898, during the Spanish–American War in Cuba, Dr. William C. Gorgas was performing surgery when the lights went out. Gorgas finished the operation with only the light cast by a jar of fireflies!

Prey for a Cure

The venom used by scorpions to paralyze their prey will soon be used in human tests in an effort to cure patients of deadly brain tumors. The venom affects the electrical activity of cancer cells and seems to stop the tumors from growing!

Little Miss Muffet was a real person! She was the daughter of Dr. Thomas Muffet, a 19th-century expert on spiders who treated her illnesses with medicines made from spiders.

Mummy Knows Best

In 12th-century Europe, the skin of ancient Egyptian mummies was boiled, ground up, and used as medicine!

Ribbit-ing Discovery

Dr. Michael A. Zasloff discovered that *magainins,* a substance found in the skin of African clawed frogs, helps fight infection! And Abbott Laboratories in Chicago, Illinois, has developed a painkiller 200 times stronger than morphine from the deadly poison secreted by the tiny phantasmal poison frog (right) found in Ecuador.

Crazy Cures

Really Steamed

Sonmez Yikilmaz was sound asleep in his tent when a snake crawled into his open mouth and slithered down his throat. The next day, an X ray showed that the snake was still alive. Instead of surgery, Yikilmaz tried an ancient snake removal remedy. He hung upside down over a bowl of steaming hot milk until, drawn by the smell, the snake slithered back out through his mouth!

Moonstruck

An early remedy for toothaches was to wait for a full moon, head to a graveyard at midnight, then rub a molar from a murdered man on the aching tooth!

Streetside Manner

The ancient Babylonians often placed sickbeds in the street so passersby could offer medical advice!

Digest This

In Louisiana during the 1800s, a tea made of cockroaches was used as a remedy for tetanus, and cockroaches fried in oil with garlic were used to cure indigestion.

SOCK IT TO ME!

In Indiana during the 19th century, a folk remedy for a head cold was to inhale the smell from a dirty sock nine times!

RIPLEY FILE: 6.12.60

The cure that can be fatal!
In the Austrian Alps, the golden primrose is sought by mountain climbers who believe it's a remedy for vertigo. Unfortunately, seeking it at such heights has led many people to their death!

Getting an Earful

In France, an early treatment for deafness was to pour the blood of a mole into the patient's ear!

Spare Parts

Feeling Chipper

Computer whiz Derek Jacobs (center) is a big fan of technology. At age 14, he convinced his family to be the first to have a rice-sized device called a VeriChip implanted in their arms. In an emergency, doctors can simply scan the chip to learn a patient's medical history, including such life-saving information as whether they are allergic to any medicines.

IRON GRIP

The first artificial limb was an iron hand ordered more than 650 years ago by Robert the Bruce, king of Scotland. Each finger could be moved by pressing a button.

Joint Venture

Jane Bhor of Duke University in Durham, North Carolina, uses the plastic knee joints of Barbie dolls to make knuckles for prosthetic fingers.

Making Faces

Robert Barron's basement is now a laboratory where he spends a lot of time making prosthetic devices, such as ears, noses, and even full faces out of soft, durable materials. Barron's painstaking attention to detail, painting the tiny veins found in ears, the freckles on noses, and the minute striations found on hands, results in replicas that look almost as good as the originals.

Barron (right) had a lot of practice altering identities in his 24-year career as an advanced disguise expert with the CIA. But since 1993, Barron has had a second career. Working closely with physicians, Barron mixes art and science to help people who have been disfigured by accident or illness.

Phoenix police officer Jason Schechterle is one of those survivors. Schechterle was severely burned when his patrol car burst into flames after being hit by a cab. He recovered, but the resulting scars not only caused stares, but affected his vision, hearing, and speech. Barron's work has changed all that. Schechterle's new nose will keep the mucous membranes from drying out and improve his speech. Ears improve his hearing by 20 percent, as well as allow him to wear glasses. Between his own indomitable spirit and Barron's artistry, Schecterle is able to lead a very fulfilling life.

Medical Marvels

Rainbow Connection

Have you heard of extrasensory perception, better known as ESP? Well, there's another form of perception that's just as extraordinary. It's called *synesthesia*. People with synesthesia see newsprint in bursts of color, taste flavors as shapes, and hear spoken language in all the colors of the rainbow! Synesthesia is considered a brain disorder, but people who have it are often surprised to discover that not everyone's world is as colorful as theirs!

WHAT A KICK!

Antonio José Herrera of Albuquerque, New Mexico, grew a third set of teeth after his second set was kicked out by a horse when he was ten years old.

Crazy Legs

In the 1930s, Francesco Lentini of Sicily, Italy, was a master musician. He was also a renowned soccer player. Perhaps having three legs contributed to his success on the field.

Stick It to Me!

Seventy-one-year-old Liew Thow Lin (below) of Gunung Rapat, Malaysia, can lift more than 60 pounds attached to a metal plate placed against his stomach. No, it's not attached in any way. Metal simply sticks to Lin's skin. Lin often appears in Malaysian newspapers, looking like a walking hardware store, with nuts, bolts, and tools dangling from his bare chest. In 2001, he pulled a car for several yards that was hooked to a chain attached to a plate stuck on his chest.

Even though Lin has been dubbed "Mr. Magnet" and "Magnet Man," Dr. Mohamed Amin says Lin's ability has nothing to do with magnetic properties, but with the fact that Lin's "skin has a special suction effect that can help metal stick to it." Apparently, the condition is genetic—all three of Lin's sons and two grandchildren have the same ability!

Extra! Extra!

DOWNRIGHT EAR-Y

British surgeons grafted Patrick Neary's severed right ear onto his thigh in an effort to regenerate the ear before reattaching it.

HICKORY-DICKORY-DOCK

After 82-year-old Frederic Green of California was pronounced dead, he was revived by the flashbulb of a coroner's camera! Hannah Beswick of England made sure that wouldn't happen to her. In her will, she left instructions that her body be regularly inspected for signs of life—so her doctor had her body placed inside a hollow grandfather clock for easy viewing.

FOREST STUMP

In 1993, when Donald Wyman of Punxsutawney, Pennsylvania, became trapped under a tree while working in the forest, he amputated his own leg with a pocketknife, then drove himself two miles to get help.

ACHOO!

Did you know that the drops of moisture in a sneeze can travel up to 150 feet per second? That's 102 miles per hour!

WOULD YOU BELIEVE?

If the DNA elements that make up a single human cell were written in 12-point type, the letter string would stretch more than 10,000 miles.

PAY NOW, DIE LATER

In the 18th century, Saint Bartholomew's Hospital i[n] London, England, charge[d] incoming patients a buria[l] fee. It was refundable if they recovered.

BIONIC GLASSES

Harold Churchey of Baltimore, Maryland, was able to see for the first time in 15 years, thanks to a miniature video camera attached to his eyeglasses that beamed electrical impulses to a surgically implanted microchip.

HEADS AND TAILS

When Valentin Grimaldo of Texas was bitten by a coral snake, he killed the poisonous reptile by biting off its head. He then tied the snake's body around his wound as a tourniquet to save his life.

ON THE FLY

In cases where gangrene and chronic infection have set in, hungry fly larvae can often save a limb from amputation. The tiny maggots eat away at dead tissue with a precision finer than any surgical instrument and, because of their voracious appetites, do an extremely thorough job. However, if the maggots aren't removed within 72 hours, they turn into flies!

BULLETPROOF SURGERY

In Bogotá, Colombia, Dr. Ricardo Uribe donned a bulletproof vest before performing surgery to remove a live grenade from the leg of soldier Nicolas Sanchez.

A STITCH IN TIME!

While stuck in a traffic jam, Dr. Ira Kahn of Beirut, Lebanon, successfully performed surgery on himself to remove his inflamed appendix!

KEYSTONE SURGERY

In 1651, Jan Doot, a Dutch locksmith, operated on himself with a kitchen knife to remove a four-ounce kidney stone.

6

WILD
THINGS

AWESOME ANIMALS AND THEIR AMAZING WAYS

Take That!

Leaping Lizards

Predators find the frilled lizard hard to spot because it looks a lot like the bark that it sits on. But when camouflage doesn't work, the lizard rears up and unfolds its fierce-looking frill to scare off enemies. Sometimes it will even hiss and lunge forward to make itself look scarier.

SPITTING MAD

When under attack, the flightless bloody-nosed beetle spits out nasty-tasting blood, which scares its enemy or makes it sick, whichever comes first!

Chemical Warfare

When the bombardier beetle goes on the defensive, it shoots a toxic squirt from its backside that makes even the fiercest predators run for cover.

Tricksters

The **puss moth caterpillar** (below) is a master of disguise. Its green color helps it blend in with leaves, but if an enemy sees it, it puffs out a bright red fold of skin around its head, complete with spots that resemble two fierce-looking eyes. If the caterpillar happens to be resting on a plant with curled leaves, it raises up its front and tail ends to look like a curly leaf. If the enemy comes close, the caterpillar might also stick out its real tail and lash it like a whip. When all else fails, it sprays formic acid at its enemy from a gland under the bright red filaments in its tail. This last trick is sure to send a predator on its way.

The official state reptile of Texas is the **horned toad**—which isn't a toad but a lizard whose "horns" are actually scales on the sides and back of its head. When threatened, the lizard will first flatten itself in hopes it won't be seen. If that doesn't work, it puffs its body up to twice its normal size. Finally, the lizard will resort to its best trick—squirting blood from its eyes. Even though it's no more than five inches long, the horned toad can shoot the blood up to four feet away!

The **sea cucumber,** which lives on the ocean floor, has a real gutsy defense. When attacked, it expels its own digestive system! The attacker becomes entangled in it, and the sea cucumber goes free. Luckily, the creature is able to grow a new set of insides.

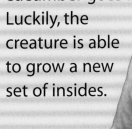

Marvelous Moms

Undercover

Although a pangolin baby can walk a few days after birth, it rides on its mother's tail instead. If the mother feels threatened, she tucks her tail—with the baby still on it—under her body. A predator would have to go through this scaly anteater's body to get to its young.

RIPLEY FILE: 5.25.69

A litter too many! **The tailless tenrec of Madagascar, which resembles a hedgehog, regularly produces the largest litters of any mammal—as many as 32 young at each birth!**

EGGS-ELLENT MAMA

The octopus stays with her eggs night and day. She won't even leave them to look for food—and can end up starving herself.

Nut Cases

Researchers observed a Japanese macaque mother calming her baby just like human mothers do. The 18-month-old monkey, who had been fussing and screaming, immediately calmed down when its mother popped an acorn into its mouth. It sucked happily for a while, then ate its pacifier. Good thing it wasn't plastic!

Mama Mia!

The mother cuckoo lays one egg in the nest of another bird species and leaves it to hatch and be raised by a foster mother. Sometimes the young cuckoo is bigger than its foster mother as well as its foster siblings, which it may even push out of the nest.

Pot Luck

The female potter wasp takes hours to fashion a little mud pot for each of her eggs. Then she finds a juicy caterpillar, paralyzes it with her stinger, and stuffs it into the pot. Once the egg hatches, the larva has a ready-made feast. Somehow, mother wasps can tell which eggs are male and which are female—and they give the males smaller pots and less food!

Dazzling Dads

Pregnant Papas

After sea horses mate, the female deposits about 100 eggs in a special pouch in the male's abdomen and swims away. It is the male's job to nourish the eggs with his body until they mature. After a month or so, the male sea horse gives birth to little sea colts!

RIPLEY FILE: 3.26.84

Safe at home! The female silvery-cheeked hornbill seals herself in a hollow tree trunk until her chicks are grown. The male feeds the family up to 20 times a day through a chink in the bark.

He's All Wet

The male sand grouse (right) flies as far as 50 miles to soak himself in water so that his young can drink from his feathers. He does this until his offspring are big enough to visit the water hole themselves.

Toe-tally Cool

After his mate lays an egg, the male emperor penguin (below) holds it on top of his toes beneath his brood flap to keep it warm. Because temperatures on the ice can dip to minus 76°F., penguin fathers huddle together to conserve body heat. It takes 64 days for the egg to hatch. Then papa penguin keeps the chick warm the same way.

Special Delivery

Male Djungarian hamsters act as midwives to their mates, helping them to give birth, then opening the babies' airways and licking them clean.

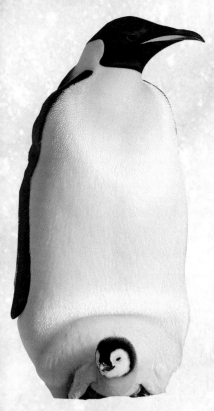

BABIES ON BOARD

The male finfoot is thought to be the only bird to fly with his chicks. How does he do it? By carrying them in special pockets under his wings.

Bon Appétit!

A Bone to Pick

Museums have discovered a secret. When it comes to cleaning organic specimens, chemicals are damaging but beetles are not. That's why beetles are employed to munch the flesh off the bones of animal carcasses. The process may be disgusting—you can hear the critters munching and the smell is foul—but no one's complaining. The bugs get to pig out, and the bare bones are left in perfect condition.

RIPLEY FILE: 4.05.65

Heavy eater! Each night, the flightless Kiwi bird of New Zealand eats its own weight in worms. This strange bird lives in a burrow, has nostrils on the end of its beak, hairlike feathers, whiskers, and no tail. It has poor eyesight, but an acute sense of smell. A kiwi is about the size of a chicken, but the female lays a big egg—one that weighs 20 percent of its own weight.

Pooper-scoopers

Dung beetles scout out fresh mammal droppings and roll the dung into a ball. Then they poke a hole in it and lay their eggs inside. When the eggs hatch, the larvae have to eat through the dung to get out.

INSTANT SLURPY

Without jaws or teeth, maggots make short work of dead animals. How? They produce a digestive juice that turns solids into liquid, spit it into their dinner, and slurp it up.

Bloodthirsty

Vampire bats bite people and other animals while they're sleeping, then lap up blood from the wounds. A vampire bat drinks more than its own weight in blood every night.

Sticks to It

The aardvark's tongue is at least a foot and a half long and coated with thick, sticky saliva—perfect for scooping up bunches of termites, its favorite food. Aardvark teeth are coated with cement. Perhaps that's why a single aardvark can grind up 50,000 termites in one night!

Beastly Brainiacs

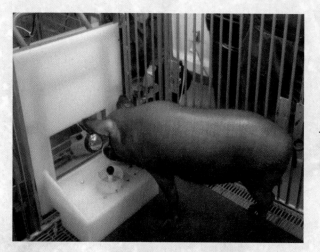

Piggin' Out

At Pennsylvania State University, Professor Stanley Curtis taught six pigs to play video games. Using their snouts to control the joysticks, they learned to match similar objects and to hit targets that get smaller and smaller. Of course, the pigs were well motivated—their efforts were instantly rewarded with M&M's.

Something to Crow About

A crow in Washington's Olympic Mountains was observed doing some creative problem solving. On the ground were several crackers that it wanted all for itself. Each time the crow picked one up and then opened its beak to get another, the first cracker fell out. The solution? The crow propped the crackers very close together in the snow, opened wide, and grabbed all seven at once!

NOSE DIVE

While hunting for food among the sharp-edged coral reefs, porpoises often cover their tender noses with face masks they fashion out of sponges.

Math-panzee

One day, Dr. Sally Boysen (above), a scientist at Ohio State University, dropped three peaches in one box and three in another. She took out number cards and asked Sheba, a chimpanzee, how many peaches were in the boxes. Sheba pointed to six. Boysen was astounded. Though Sheba had been taught to recognize numbers, she'd never been taught to count or add!

RIPLEY FILE: 9.11.77

Monkey see, monkey do! A chimpanzee named Lucy learned sign language, acquiring a vocabulary of 80 words.

Mud-packers

Work elephants in Myanmar (formerly Burma) have been known to stuff the bells hanging around their neck with mud. Why? So the bells won't ring when the elephants sneak out at night to steal the bananas they love to eat.

Heroic Tales

Smoke Detector

When actor Drew Barrymore's house caught on fire in February 2001, she was sound asleep in her bedroom. It's a good thing Flossie, Barrymore's Labrador retriever–chow mix, awakened her in time for her to escape.

Pig Tale

On the day two burglars forced their way into Rebecca Moyer's home, her 200-pound pet pig was taking a snooze in the kitchen. When Arnold (left) heard his owner scream, he came to the rescue, chomping on one of the bad guy's legs— and sending both crooks scurrying away in fear.

Winging It

A woman in Hermitage, Tennessee, who fell and cut her head, was rescued after her pet canary, Bibs, flew down the road to alert her niece. The bird kept tapping on the niece's window until she followed it to the accident scene.

PEG LEG

A pigeon named Cher Ami carried messages that saved an American battalion during World War I. It was shot while flying over enemy lines and was later fitted with a wooden leg.

RIPLEY FILE: 9.12.65

On the rocks! In 1919, the S.S. *Ethie*, a 414-ton steamship, ran aground off Newfoundland, Canada, during a violent storm. With the ship breaking up in heavy seas, a Newfoundland dog gripped a lifeline in its teeth and swam to the beach, where a bystander secured the line. All 92 passengers and crew were pulled to safety.

He-roo

A baby kangaroo rescued by Nigel Etherington of Perth, Australia, later saved Etherington from a fire by banging its tail on his door until he awoke and escaped.

Creature Comforts

No Horsing Around

Cuddles (right), a miniature horse just two feet tall, is the first guide horse for the blind in the United States. Cuddles's training by the Guide Horse Foundation was put to the test in New York City. Clad in tiny sneakers to keep her from slipping, Cuddles took the busy streets and noisy subways in stride.

Seizing the Moment!

Because people with epilepsy often lose control of their body during a seizure, it's important for them to be somewhere safe when a seizure occurs. Epileptics have no idea when a seizure will strike, but research shows that dogs do. How they know about a seizure beforehand remains a mystery, but dogs like Brian Revheim's English setter, Arthur (left), can be trained to alert their owner minutes before an attack takes place.

Sheep Shearers

In 1917, as part of the World War I conservation effort, sheep were used to trim the White House lawn. ti b

The path to cleanliness! An elephant owned by England's Duke of Devonshire was trained to wet down the paths of a park with a watering can and then sweep them with a broom.

Bird's-eye View

Homing pigeons equipped with tiny aluminum cameras were used by both sides during World War II to photograph areas too heavily fortified to be flown over by planes. The cameras were activated by air rushing through a rubber ball.

WIRED

A ferret named Misty was used by the United States Space Command in Colorado to help rewire a new computerized command center.

Extra! Extra!

HISS!
Burrowing owls imitate the sounds of rattlesnakes in order to scare off predators.

NOSING AROUND
The California sea lion uses its nose as bait to capture sea gulls.

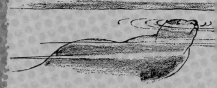

WAY DOWN UNDER
In December 2000, it took six men with a wheelbarrow to drag a rare 110-pound alligator snapping turtle out of a sewer beneath the streets of Sydney, Australia. In 1982, eight baby snappers were stolen from a reptile park. If this turtle was one of them, he had a long time to grow in the sewers—and his friends might still be down there!

EEEEK!
At the Rat Olympics held annually at Michigan's Kalamazoo College, rodents compete in such events as the broad jump, the tightrope walk, and soccer!

I SPY
At the University of California's Joseph M. Long Marine Laboratory, four sea lions have been trained to videotape gray whales.

HOLD THE BEEF
The largest and strongest animals on Earth do not eat meat. Elephants, gorillas, hippopotamuses, giraffes, rhinoceroses, water buffalo, and musk oxen are all vegetarians.

SALT OF THE EARTH

The petrel, a small seabird, drinks only seawater. If left inland beside a body of freshwater, it will die of thirst.

IN THE PINK

Snowflake, a gorilla captured in Africa in 1967, was an albino with white hair, pink skin, and blue eyes.

THE DIE IS CAST

The highly poisonous boxfish is also called a dicefish because of its square shape and multiple spots. As a new arrival to Britain's Bournemouth Oceanarium, a boxfish named Dotty was seriously stressed and was releasing so much venom, the staff feared she'd poison herself. So they put a real die—about the same size as the young Dotty—into the tank, hoping she'd think it was another boxfish. It worked. Now that she has some company, Dotty has stopped releasing venom.

LITTLE MAMA

After an elephant named Jubalani was abandoned by its biological mother, it was adopted by a sheep named Skaap, at a wildlife refuge in South Africa.

SLIMED!

When pursued by a hawk, the houbara bustard, an Asian desert bird, sprays its foe's eyes and feathers with a thick sticky fluid that blinds and disables it.

SHOWING HIS METAL

In Germany, a stork named Peter, who lost his beak in a fight, was fitted with an aluminum replacement.

POWER SPRAYERS

The civet, a catlike animal found in Africa and Asia, drives off its enemies with a foul-smelling spray. This is actually used in the manufacture of some perfumes. *Pee-yew!*

93

7

WACKY
WONDERS

ASTONISHING STRUCTURES AND PECULIAR PLACES

Daffy Dwellings

Website

New homeowners Susan and Andrew Parker had no idea they'd bought a comic book landmark—until they started getting mail addressed to Spider-Man! It seems their address in Forest Hills, New York, is the same as the comic book hero's. Not only that— the surname of Spider-Man's alter ego is Parker! Go figure!

Rock Solid

While delivering mail in rural France in 1879, Ferdinand Cheval stumbled over a stone fancifully eroded by wind and water. Inspired by the beauty of the stone, Cheval decided to construct a home from the same material. It took him 33 years of hauling mortar and limestone to create *Le Palais Idéal* (right), a four-story, 86-foot-long castle covered with intricate carvings of animals, plants, and people.

LID FLIPPER

Felix Famularo decorated the front porch of his home in Picayune, Mississippi, with more than 79,000 metal pop-top tabs!

Jet-sitters

Marcus Sitticus, the 17th-century prince-archbishop of Salzburg, Austria, had water jets installed on the stools around his palace courtyard (above) in order to surprise his unsuspecting guests. Four hundred years later, they still work!

RIPLEY FILE: 4.18.43

At home with recycling! Constructed from an endless variety of found objects, a house in Ballarat, Australia, resembles nothing more than a colorful patchwork quilt. Some of the materials used include lamps, jugs, dishes, shells, rocks, ornaments, and broken glass.

Spirited Retreats

Phantom Tantrums

Chingle Hall (right), the oldest surviving brick house in Great Britain, was built in 1260 by Adam de Singleton. The home's other claim to fame is its resident poltergeist. Not content to float through walls, the phantom has a reputation for throwing dishes and other household objects at visitors.

Going Nowhere

Sarah Winchester had stairways that run into the ceiling and doors that open onto blank walls built into her 160-room mansion in San Jose, California. Why? To soothe the spirits of people who were killed by rifles made by her late husband's family. Winchester believed she would only live as long as she kept building. Construction continued 24 hours a day for 38 years—until 1922, when she died.

SPIRIT OF THE LAW

In 1991, an appeals court in New York State officially declared a house in Nyack, New York, to be haunted!

Tower of Terror

Fifteen-year-old James Froggatt (left) and his younger brother and sister live in a small row house inside the Tower of London grounds. Their father works there as one of the guards, who are also known as "beefeaters." Why? Because at one time the Tower guards were rewarded with daily rations of meat as part of their wages. These days they get paychecks instead.

The Tower of London, built by William the Conqueror in 1066, is one of the most popular tourist attractions in England. Famous for its former function as a prison and execution site, the Tower is equally famous for being haunted by the souls of dead prisoners. Well-versed in the history of the Tower, the Froggatt children enjoy entertaining visitors with the tales of terror that make up a large part of Tower lore.

Important prisoners were once held in a part of the Tower called the Queen's House. Anne Boleyn, the second wife of King Henry VIII, was housed there before she was beheaded. Some think she has never really left. People who have stayed overnight claim to have felt her hands on their neck.

Wacky Galleries

Bug Theater

Based on the premise that there's no roach like a dead roach, the Cockroach Hall of Fame Museum exhibits the dead bugs dressed in costumes and posed in mini dioramas. Marilyn Monroach (top right) and Ross Peroach (near right) are two of the museum's biggest crowd pleasers.

HAIRPIECES

In Missouri's Hair Museum, items made entirely from hair—including wreaths, bookmarks, and a diary—show that 19th-century cosmetology schools didn't let hair clippings go to waste.

Museum of Madness

At Minnesota's Glore Psychiatric Museum, visitors can view such memorable exhibits as the contents (above) found in a deceased patient's stomach—1,446 pieces of metal, including nails, hairpins, buttons, safety pins, screws, and bolts!

Out of the Odd-inary

Robert Ripley opened his first Odditorium at the 1933 Chicago World's Fair. Many people fainted at the sight of contortionists, magicians, fireproof people, and razor-blade eaters—but that did not stop them from coming back for more! The first Odditoriums were such a success that in 1939, Ripley opened a permanent one in New York City.

Today, Ripley Odditoriums are more popular than ever. Instead of live performers, there are wax replicas of the legendary greats. Each Odditorium features hundreds of unbelievable exhibits, incredible illusions, and film clips of amazing stunts. The video of Dagmarr Rothman swallowing a mouse and bringing the unharmed creature back up from his stomach is a particular crowd pleaser.

The museums are filled with scores of curiosities scooped up from all corners of the world. Among the most popular exhibits are shrunken head and skull collections. Now you have a better chance than ever to see them in person, since Odditoriums can be found all across America and in many other countries as well.

Amazing Structures

Bridge to the Future

In 1502, Leonardo da Vinci drew up plans for a bridge to connect the European and Asian sides of Istanbul, Turkey. But the bridge was never built because the Turkish ruler thought the design was an architectural impossibility. Five hundred years later, in 2001, the plans were rediscovered by artist Vebjørn Sand who was able to get the bridge built in As, Norway. Sand hopes to build a Leonardo-style bridge on every continent as a symbol that "you can make anything you dream a reality."

Pachyderm Pavilion

Built in 1882 by James T. Lafferty, this historical landmark shaped like an elephant—named Lucy by the residents of Margate, New Jersey—is 65 feet tall and weighs 90 tons. For four dollars, you can wander though its pink rooms and get an elephant's-eye view of the city.

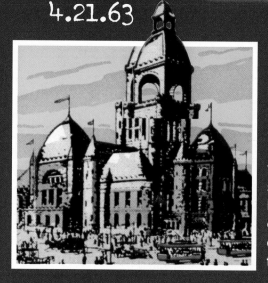

The Coal Palace! Built out of coal, this structure was erected in 1890 to promote Iowa as a coal-producing state. Featuring a dance floor, auditorium, and 30-foot waterfall, it was 230 feet long and 130 feet wide with a 200-foot tower. It's a shame such a magnificent building had to be dismantled. But once the exposition was over, it was taken down because coal is such a flammable substance.

It's Melting!

A building in Odeillo, France, which was designed to tap solar energy for heat and light, looks as if it's actually dissolving.

MAKING HAY

In 2002, four ninth-graders from the Crow reservation in Montana won $25,000 for their Earth-friendly design for a community center made with concrete-covered bales of hay—which provide built-in insulation.

Out-landish

Rock-etry

In 1916, ranchers drilling a well in Nevada accidentally pierced a vein of boiling hot water, and Fly Geyser (below) has been gushing ever since. Over the years, minerals from the spouting water have built up, forming three hills that look like 15-foot-high termite mounds. Their bright colors are produced by a combination of minerals, algae, and bacteria.

Cheers!

Marvelously wrought in stone by the lathe-work action of the wind, the 15-foot-high Goblet of Venus (left) in San Juan County, Utah, stood on a base 10 inches wide—before it was destroyed by vandals, that is.

Coal Coast

One of the most beautiful beaches in the world can be found in Hawaii, where turquoise waves crash over glistening jet-black sand made of disintegrated volcanic lava.

The Seated Woman, a natural rock sculpture near Manisa, Turkey, has appeared to be shedding tears for 2,000 years. Her tears are formed by springs of water hidden beneath the rock.

RIPLEY FILE: 11.24.46

The great lake of soda! Magadi Lake in Kenya, Africa, is 20 miles long and two miles wide. Minerals from the volcanic springs that supply it form a thick crust of carbonate of soda, which is dredged up and made into soda ash for use in glass-making.

Worth Its Salt

Photographers come from far and wide to capture the surreal vision of Bolivia's Lake Uyuni. The world's largest salt lake, it is only six to 20 inches at its deepest. Cloudlike salt formations jutting out of the azure water make it hard to distinguish lake from sky.

Extra! Extra!

HORNING IN
The archway at the entrance to City Center Park in Jackson, Wyoming, is constructed entirely of elk antlers.

REMOTE CONTROL
Computer wizard Bill Gates lives in an automated house. He can fill the bathtub in his master bathroom and regulate the temperature and water level while he's driving home from work!

SHOE-IN
Marcel and Maureen Lauberte, of Corona, California, have a house that stands 14 feet tall, is 23 feet long, and is built in the shape of a shoe.

WORLD'S FLATTEST FLAT
A family of five in Alexandria, Egypt, lives in three rooms hung on a wall of another building.

SHAPING UP
An odd-shaped castle tower in Oxford, England, was built in accordance with instructions that it could not be round, square, oval, or oblong.

SUSPENDED ANIMATION
Almost destroyed in battle more than 300 years ago, a castle in Bridgnorth, England, tilts at three times the angle of the Leaning Tower of Pisa.

MONSTERS AND DEMONS AND FIENDS—OH, MY!

Instead of trees, flowers, and fountains, the garden of Bomarzo near Viterbo, Italy, has monstrous statues carved from solid rock. One face is so large, a person can walk into its mouth.

OFF WITH THEIR HEADS

Statues in ancient Rome were often made with detachable heads, which could be removed and replaced with the heads of more popular personalities.

SOMETIMES YOU FEEL LIKE A NUT

The Nut Museum, founded by Elizabeth Tashjian in Connecticut, exhibits nuts of every kind from all over the world, including a 35-pound coco-de-mer, also called a double coconut.

NO BULL!

An office building in Turlock, California, was designed to look like a giant bulldozer.

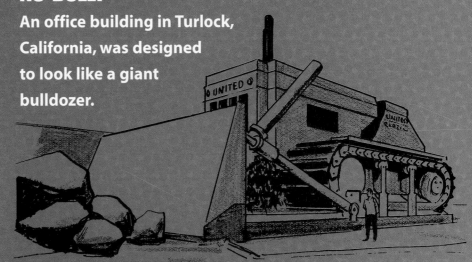

SLEEPLESS IN ZURICH

For 900 years, no one has been able to stay overnight at a Hapsburg castle near Zurich, Switzerland. Why? Because the ghost of a murdered woman still screams in terror every single night. As recently as 1978, a nonbeliever named Horst Von Roth tried to stay the night but fled the haunted dwelling in horror.

ALL KEYED UP

Every doorway in the village of Mogroum, Chad, Africa, is shaped like a keyhole in the belief it will keep out unwanted visitors.

8

OUTRAGEOUS!

ODD FELLOWS, ODD JOBS, AND INCREDIBLE KIDS

Body Language

Body of Art

Charles Wagner (right) invented a revolutionary tattooing machine in 1904 and is still considered the godfather of tattoo art. His lavish tattoos included a trio of horses on his chest that was copied from a painting by French artist Rosa Bonheur, and a scene titled "A Trip to Mars" on his back.

Lizard of Odds

Eric Sprague's love of reptiles prompted him to do his best to look like one (left). He had himself tattooed with scales from head to toe. These, along with his surgically split tongue and the bony ridge set into his forehead, have allowed him to achieve his goal.

RIPLEY FILE: 6.10.45

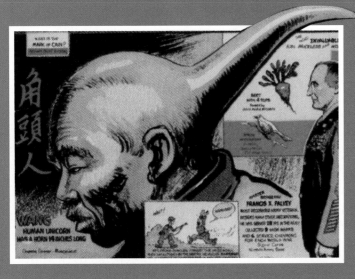

The amazing unicorn man! In 1928, Robert Ripley was shown a photograph of Weng, a Manchurian farmer who had a 13-inch horn on the back of his head. Weng, featured in this 1945 cartoon, made a major impression on Ripley. Afterward, whenever he traveled the world, he searched for other people with unusual features or abilities.

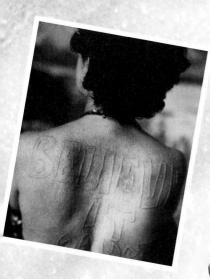

Human Slate

Rosa Barthelme could raise temporary welts on her skin by drawing on it with a blunt instrument.

SIGN ME UP!

Former boxer Dick Hyland was "signed" with the tattooed names of more than 600 celebrities, friends, and acquaintances. Ripley's name can be found in the center of Hyland's chest, right above Pancho Villa's.

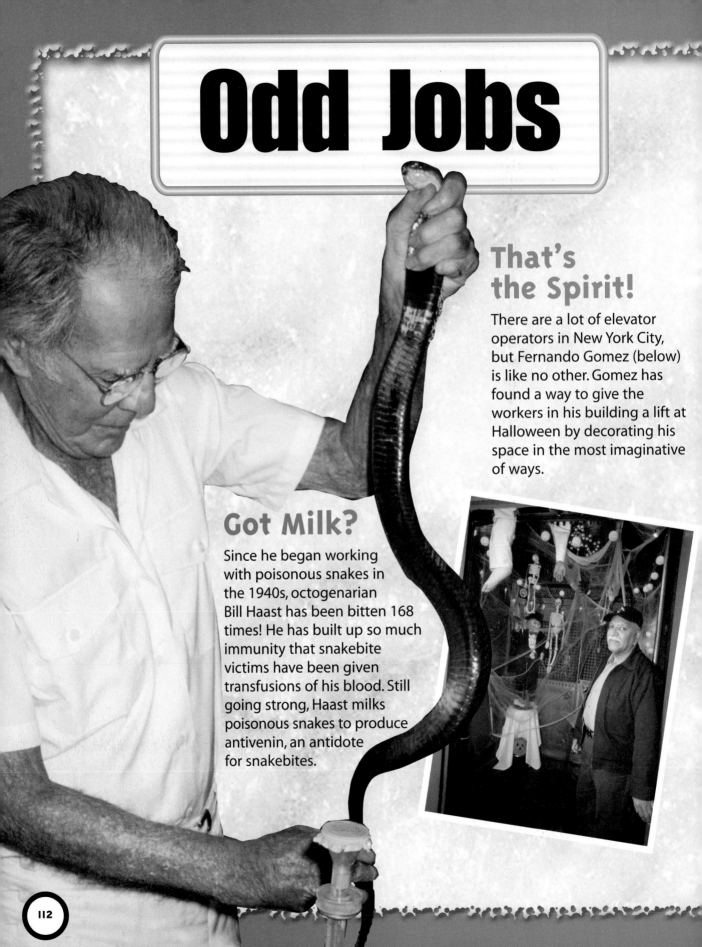

Odd Jobs

That's the Spirit!

There are a lot of elevator operators in New York City, but Fernando Gomez (below) is like no other. Gomez has found a way to give the workers in his building a lift at Halloween by decorating his space in the most imaginative of ways.

Got Milk?

Since he began working with poisonous snakes in the 1940s, octogenarian Bill Haast has been bitten 168 times! He has built up so much immunity that snakebite victims have been given transfusions of his blood. Still going strong, Haast milks poisonous snakes to produce antivenin, an antidote for snakebites.

RIPLEY FILE: 9.08.40

Failed singer turns pirate! Frustrated in his ambition to be a vocalist, Benito sought revenge on the high seas. He became a pirate and was such a scoundrel, he earned the title Benito of the Bloody Sword. In 1820, he looted the *Mary Dier* of treasure it was taking from Peru to Spain. The treasure, which today would be worth more than $300,000,000, is said to be buried on Cocos Island near Panama, where it is still waiting to be discovered.

Sweet Deal

In 2002, Fortnum & Mason, one of Britain's fanciest grocery stores, advertised for a chocolate taster at a salary equal to $54,000 a year. To earn his or her pay, a taster must travel the world sampling as much chocolate as possible. It's a tough job, but somebody has to do it!

Dollars and Scents

Scientists at the University of Illinois are looking for ways to freshen the air around pig farms. Would feeding them different types of food improve the atmosphere? To find out, they paid people to sniff the results. When these people say their job stinks, they're not kidding!

IT'S A DOG'S LIFE!

Professional food taster Edwin Rose of Hayes, England, taste-tests cat and dog foods for a living.

Flaky Folk

Shelled Out

Camillo Russo of Melbourne, Australia, loves seashells so much that he uses them to decorate his clothing and his home, which is covered with more than a million seashells!

Am I Blue?

In 1999, Stan Jones, Montana's 2002 Libertarian candidate for the Senate, was worried that chaotic conditions related to Y2K might interfere with antibiotic supplies. So he started taking colloidal silver, which is marketed as an antibacterial agent and immunity booster. An unfortunate side effect? Blue skin!

Above It All

In 1929, C. A. Traff, known as the best one-legged athlete in the United States, got around on crutches that were 11 feet long.

Florence Nightingale (1820–1910), the founder of modern nursing, always carried a pet owl in her pocket!

RIPLEY FILE: 4.28.40

Keeping up appearances! Antonin-Nompar de Caumont La Force (1633–1723), the Duke of Lauzun and Marshal of France, never wore the same outfit twice. Although King Louis XIV imprisoned La Force for ten years to keep him from marrying the richest heiress in Europe, La Force still changed his wig, hat, shoes, and cloak every day!

A Real Eyepopper

Avelino Perez got his kicks by popping his eyes in and out of their sockets.

That's Entertainment

Hooked on Danger

Criss Angel, a magician, once spent six hours dangling from a ceiling on fishhooks (above). In 2002, shackled in chains and wearing a scubalike breathing mechanism, Angel submerged himself upside down for 24 hours in a 220-gallon tank of water in New York City's Times Square.

One Cool Guy

In November 2000, street magician David Blaine (left) executed his most amazing stunt ever. With doctors standing by to monitor his condition, Blaine spent just under 62 hours inside a six-ton block of ice on the corner of 44th Street and Broadway in New York City.

RIPLEY FILE: 11.22.64

Gave a strong performance! German circus performer Miss Heliot entertained audiences in 1953 by carrying a 660-pound lion on her shoulders.

Multitasking

Jackie Gross of Boston, Massachusetts, could whistle harmony while playing the harmonica with his nose.

Twisted

In 1937, Alma Ynclan, a child contortionist from Tampa, Florida, executed her version of a pretzel.

LOONY TUNES

F. G. Holt of Arkansas had such good control of his facial muscles that he could play a medley of tunes with bells attached to his eyebrows.

Kid Power

Labor of Love

At the age of 12, Craig Kielburger read about a boy in Pakistan who had to begin working in a carpet factory at the age of four. Craig was so affected by the story that he started Free the Children, an organization whose purpose is to free children from exploitation and teach them how to take action for themselves.

The Write Stuff

When 12-year-old Kenya Jordana James couldn't find a magazine that featured girls just like her, she created her own—*Blackgirl Magazine,* which deals with all aspects of African-American teen life.

FLOWER CHILD

Olivia Bennett's been painting flowers since she was old enough to hold a crayon. These days, her paintings sell for up to $15,000! Not bad for someone who just turned 13!

Going Places

reg Smith is a pint-sized dynamo with a huge IQ and an even bigger heart. Before he was two, Greg could name all the dinosaurs that ever lived. At the age of nine, he graduated from high school with honors, and in May 2003 at age 13, he graduated from Randolph-Macon College in Virginia.

Greg uses his time off to help children whose lives have been scarred by violence and poverty.

In July 2001, as the founder of International Youth Advocates, an organization that lobbies on behalf of underprivileged children, Greg attended the groundbreaking ceremony of the Amani School in Kenya, Africa, where 600 children of three rival nomadic tribes will attend school together.

Due to Greg's efforts, and the help of President Bill Clinton, January 1 has been designated an international holiday for peace. No doubt that is why, at the age of 13, Greg Smith is the youngest person ever to be nominated for the Nobel Peace Prize. Way to go, Greg!

Extra! Extra!

ROYAL HEAD HOLDER

Britain's King John (1199–1216) had a servant whose official job was to hold the king's head if the monarch became seasick.

URP!

BIG COVER-UP

G. Clifford Prout, Jr., president of the Society Against Indecency to Naked Animals, left $400,000 in his will to be spent on clothes for animals.

FEELING SHEEPISH

Jake Manglewurzel of Yorkshire, England, regularly lectured from a pulpit on top of his farmhouse about the evils of conformity—to a flock of sheep!

CHIMP CHANGE

When an elderly Danish woman died, she left her entire life savings to her loved ones. As a result, six chimpanzees at the Copenhagen Zoo were suddenly $60,000 richer! Now, that's a lot of bananas!

MAKING A STINK

Nine-year-old Danny Denault of New Milford, Connecticut, was the proud winner of a $500 prize in a Rotten Sneaker Contest sponsored by Odor Eaters. Asked the secret of his success, Danny had a quick response. "Cow pies," he replied. "They're just hard to avoid. They're everywhere."

ON FILE

Renda Long of Glendale, Arizona, started growing her fingernails in 1974. By 1985, her longest nail had reached 14.5 inches while the shortest was a mere 8.5 inches.

HANDY TALENT

Zelma George (below) of Canton, Ohio, could write forward, backward, upside down, backward and upside down, and also write a different sentence with each hand in any combination simultaneously. Whew!

GOLDEN OLDIE

Marta Aurenes is the new bouncer at a pub in Oslo, Norway. To keep fit, she works out with weights three times a week and is enrolled in a police-training course for bouncers. Not bad for a 91-year-old grandmother!

DOUBLE TALK

Lord Dudley and Ward (1781–1883), British foreign secretary in 1827, was certain that his two titles made him twins. He talked to himself constantly—using a falsetto voice for Dudley and a bass voice for Ward.

RISING STAR

Thirteen-year-old Chaille Stoval has made four documentaries for HBO. The youngest reporter in the Press Corps, he was granted interviews by both the Democratic and the Republican presidential candidates in the 2000 election. Already nominated for a prime-time Emmy, Chaille is the youngest director ever to sign a feature film contract. His budget? $2,000,000!

HANGING IN

Albert J. Smith (right), a one-armed wallpaper-hanger from Dedham, Massachusetts, worked on Robert Ripley's office in the Empire State Building in New York City.

AMAZING MASON

Willie Boular of Atchison, Kansas, who was deaf, mute, and without legs, laid 46,000 paving bricks in less than eight hours.

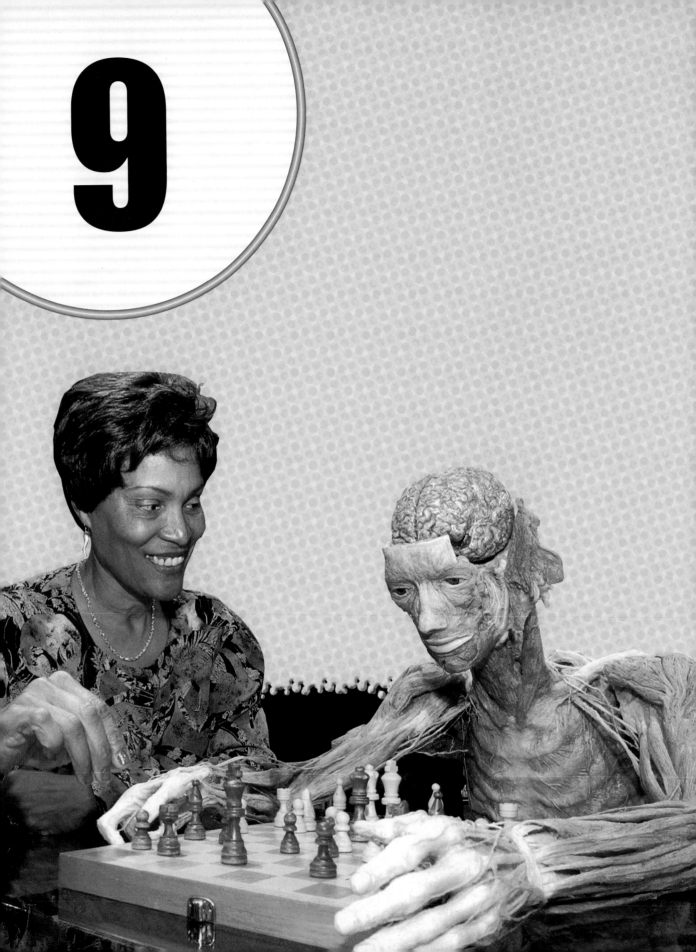

9

FREAKY!

BODIES, BONES, AND TWISTS OF FATE

Would You Believe?

Come Again?

Meet Lorraine and Loretta Szymanski of Pittsburgh, Pennsylavania—and Lorraine and Loretta Szymanski of Pittsburgh, Pennsylvania! Both sets of twins attended the same school, were in the same class, and lived in the same neighborhood, but were not related in any way!

SPECIAL DELIVERIES

Isabella, Matthew, and Riley Bradbury and their great-grandmother may be different ages, but they all share the same birthday: September 1. The chances of this happening? One in 48 million!

Bonding Experience

Actor Sean Connery, who played the film character James Bond, was once stopped for a traffic violation by police officer Sergeant James Bond.

Twist of Fate

As Jack and Colleen de Vries flipped through photographs of children to adopt, they kept going back to a four-year-old boy with a big smile. Soon the de Vries were on a plane bound for Russia where Dimitri, Dima for short, lived at the Orphipsky orphanage.

By the time they were ready to go back to the United States, Dimitri and his adopted parents already felt like family. The only drawback was that Dima had to leave a loved one behind—a little girl named Nastia who was like a sister to him.

Dima happily adjusted to his new home in Grand Rapids, Michigan. But each night when his parents would come to kiss him good night, he would say, "Nastia, America." The de Vries tried to adopt Nastia, too, but were told that her mother, who was unable to care for her, would not give her permission.

The years went by and another adoptive couple who lived in Grand Rapids fell in love with Nastia's

photo. Because her mother had died, they were able to adopt Nastia. When they brought her home, they gave her a doll that she named Dima. No one knew the significance of the name until one evening when Dimitri and his parents were having dinner at the hospital where Mrs. de Vries worked. In the booth behind them, a little voice was speaking Russian. It was Nastia! The overjoyed children had found each other!

Organ-ized!

Creepy Corpses

German professor Gunther von Hagens has created an elaborate public anatomy lesson with his traveling exhibit of donated human corpses in active poses, such as running and playing games. The bodies, minus their skin, are preserved by *plastination*, a process that involves replacing bodily fluids with plastics. Diseased body parts are also exhibited alongside healthy specimens. By comparing a healthy set of lungs with those of a smoker, von Hagens says, "You can decide if you really want to smoke."

Show and Tell

In 1997, pathologist Dr. Thomas Harvey placed the brain of Albert Einstein in a Tupperware container and drove it from Florida to California to show it to the dead scientist's granddaughter.

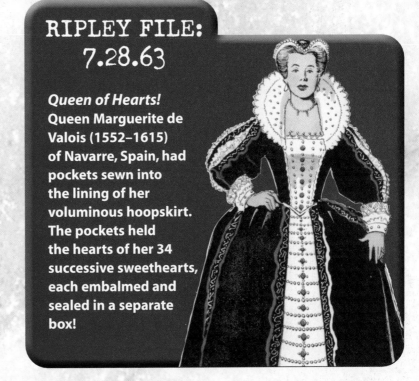

Queen of Hearts! Queen Marguerite de Valois (1552–1615) of Navarre, Spain, had pockets sewn into the lining of her voluminous hoopskirt. The pockets held the hearts of her 34 successive sweethearts, each embalmed and sealed in a separate box!

Finger Bowl

The middle finger of the right hand of Galileo (1564–1642), astronomer and inventor of the telescope, is displayed in the Museum of the History of Science, in Florence, Italy.

CONSTANT COMPANION

When King Philip I of Spain died in 1506, Queen Juana had her husband's body embalmed and placed in a jeweled coffin that she kept by her side while she ate and slept.

Bizarre Burials

Car-cass

In 1998, at the age of 84, Rose Martin of Tiverton, Massachusetts, was buried in her 1962 Corvair (above). She'd bought it new for $2,500 and had decided she never wanted to be parted from it.

Stylish Ending

When opera virtuoso Enrico Caruso (left) died in 1921, his body was put on display in a transparent coffin in the Del Planto Cemetery in Naples, Italy. His clothes were regularly changed for his adoring fans! After five years, his wife had his body removed and placed in a tomb.

Fireproof

The Tlingit people of Alaska cremated their dead—except for shamans, whom they believed would not burn. Shamans were embalmed and placed in primitive shelters along with the body of a slave to serve them in the afterlife.

SPACE CADET

The ashes of Star Trek creator Gene Roddenberry were blasted into space on board a Pegasus rocket that will circle Earth for years!

RIPLEY FILE: 11.05.61

Eternal vigilance! War Eagle, chief of the Yankton Sioux Indians, was buried in Sioux City, Iowa, sitting on his horse and with his eyes just above the surface of the ground so he could continue to overlook his old hunting grounds.

Skullduggery

If you're not careful, heads will roll at the Bone Chapel in Hallstatt, Austria. Built when the cemetery behind the Catholic church got too crowded, the chapel now holds 600 skulls. Each one is painted with its name and dates and is decorated with pretty designs—ivy for the men and roses for the women.

Extra! Extra!

KEYSTONE

Concert pianist Madge Ward's gravestone in Tyler, Texas, is a 25-ton black granite grand piano.

BODY SNATCHERS

At the Paco Cemetery in Manila, Philippines, corpses are placed in chambers in the cemeter wall for an annual rental fee. If families fail to pay the fee, the remains are removed and burned.

ROOTING AROUND

When he died in 1683, religious leader Roger Williams was buried beside an apple tree in Providence, Rhode Island. The roots of the tree slowly absorbed his body and assumed a human shape!

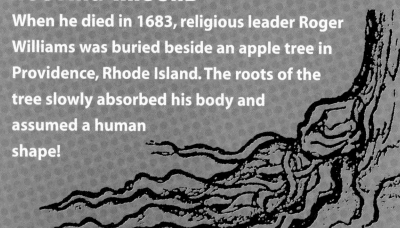

STUCK TO HIS SEA

Charlemagne, emperor o the Holy Roman Empire, on his throne for 397 yea He was interred on his marble throne in 814 C.E. after a reign of 46 years— and his corpse was still sitting there when the tomb was opened in 116!

HEARTTHROB

After the death of her husband in 1675, Madame Marguerite Therese of France carried his embalmed heart around with her in a small glass case.

UP IN SMOKE

Huge, costly effigies of white elephants were once constructed in Myanmar (formerly Burma) to be used as funeral pyres for notables and burned to the ground right along with the corpse.

TOMB OF THE UNKNOWN PLUMBER

A gravestone covered in pipes and faucets in the Main Street cemetery in Plaquemine, Louisiana, belongs to an unknown plumber who died in 1904.

SOUL FOOD

The grave of Manfred Asho, a wealthy native of Cameroon who died in 1933, is topped by a huge statue. Next to it is a table on which a meal for his soul is served each day.

DOUBLE TROUBLE

On March 6, 2002, just under two hours apart, 70-year-old twin brothers were killed in two separate accidents while riding their bicycles on the same icy highway in Finland.

ALL BOTTLED UP

In 19th-century Borneo, when a person died, the body was squeezed into a jar and kept in the house of relatives for a year prior to burial.

PREPARED FOR THE WORST

In the early 1900s, a man known as Dead Eye Jack was often spotted on the roads of Victoria, Australia, carrying a coffin on his back. Why? He used it as a bed. When it rained, Dead Eye stood the coffin upright against a tree and slept standing up inside it. As many predicted, one day he never came out!

10

ODDS
AND ENDS

POT LUCK, ODD ART, AND GOOFY GADGETS

Way to Go!

Roll, Roll, Roll Your Boat

Lyndon Yorke, inventor of a wicker car and the *Tritanic*, a tricycle catamaran, was named Best British Eccentric of 2001.

Flying Solo

Solar Trek XFV is a personal flying machine that's almost as easy to operate as a bicycle. Invented by Michael Moshier, Solar Trek has two gas-engine-powered fans that extend above the frame like giant ears. The pilot stands on a pair of footrests, tightens the body belt, and holds on to the joystick controls. With the monetary support he's getting from the Pentagon and NASA, Moshier is hoping that one day Solar Trek will be able to soar 8,000 feet at 80 miles per hour.

Slick Licks

A motorized ice-cream cone elminates the need to turn the cone while licking.

A store in Taiwan that sells bulletproof vests offers a free pair of bulletproof underpants to every customer!

RIPLEY FILE: 8.10.41

Canine power assist! A dog tricycle that reached a speed of six miles per hour was invented by a Frenchman named Guitu. The wheels were powered by two running dogs.

How Sweet It Is!

Who wouldn't love to own the Humbug-Major Sweet Machine to supply an endless amount of caramel apples and candy on demand?

Odd-inary Art

Golden Thrones

Jeweler Lam Sai-wing of Hong Kong has created the Rolls-Royce of toilets. Made out of solid gold, it is the centerpiece in a lavish bathroom whose ceiling is encrusted with rubies, sapphires, and emeralds.

Scrap-o-saurus

Jim Garry of Farmingdale, New Jersey, creates detailed dinosaur skeletons out of old car parts.

Just Ducky

Ducks, bears, armadillos, you name it! Leo Sewell creates them all from plastic and metal garbage found on the streets of Philadelphia.

RIPLEY FILE:
1.27.63

Carpet of ashes! Every year, multicolored volcanic ash is used to create a colorful design in front of the city hall of Orotava on Tenerife, the largest of the Canary Islands.

Hood Ornaments

After Tyree Guyton of Detroit, Michigan, graduated from art school, he decided to transform Heidelburg Street from a run-down neighborhood to a place of humor and hope. Guyton has turned everything from discarded vehicles to abandoned houses into works of art.

BLOCKBUSTER

Five hundred children used 200,000 plastic building blocks to build a 63-foot-tall tower in Saint Louis Park, Minnesota.

Extra! Extra!

DIAMOND-BACKED?

In 1994, a department store in Amsterdam, Holland, used four rattlesnakes to guard a display of diamonds.

ROYAL FLUSH

Self-cleaning toilets that pop up out of the ground night after other facilities have closed will soon be featured in central London. During the daytime hours, they'll be pulled back underground by remote control!

TRASH-OSAURUS

At the Children's Garbage Museum in southwest Connecticut, there is a 24-foot-long, 11-foot-tall sculpture of a dinosaur made out of trash. The one-ton work of art is equivalent to the amount of garbage each person in the United States generates every year!

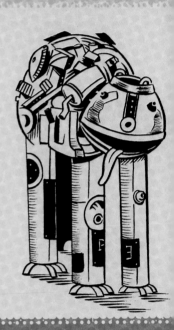

SHEDDING LIGHT

In Quemado, New Mexico, there is a Christmas tree made out of approximately 700 elk antlers covered with pretty lights (above).

SCAT CAT!

A company in Tucson, Arizona, sells software that emits a high decibel screech to scare away any cat that dares to walk across its owner's keyboard.

WAKE-UP CALL

Talk Time, a clock invented by 13-year-old Shannon Crabill, wakes you gently with a message you've recorded yourself instead of the jarring noise of an alarm.